I AM DIFFERENT!
CAN YOU FIND ME?

by MANJULA PADMANABHAN

Charlesbridge

A GLOBAL FUND FOR
Children
BOOK

Many thanks to the following native speakers and language experts: Irit Aharony, Mostafa Atamnia, Carole Bergin, Louise Burkhart, Yi Cao, Ron Daise, Chiara Frenquellucci, Lou Ann Ha'aheo Guanson, Raychelle Harris, Naseem Hines, Katherine Mille, Emily Fong Mitchell, Dov Nathanson, Gloria Nathanson, Harrison O. Oduka, Solomon Ratt, Daisy Rockwell, Angela Sanchez, James M. Taggart, Jolyon Tiglao, Nate Van Duzer, G. Oj A. Vecenti, Mary Willie, and the Global Fund for Children staff.

The Global Fund for Children (www.globalfundforchildren.org) is a nonprofit organization committed to advancing the dignity of children and youth around the world. Global Fund for Children books teach young people to value diversity and help them become productive and caring citizens of the world.

Developed by The Global Fund for Children
1101 Fourteenth Street NW, Suite 420
Washington, DC 20005
(202) 331-9003
www.globalfundforchildren.org

Published by Charlesbridge
85 Main Street
Watertown, MA 02472
(617) 926-0329
www.charlesbridge.com

First published in India by Tulika Publishers under the title
I Am Different!! Can You Find Me?
13 Prithvi Avenue
Abhiramapuram
Chennai 600 018, INDIA

Part of the proceeds from this book's sales will be donated to The Global Fund for Children to support innovative community-based organizations that serve the world's most vulnerable children and youth. Details about the donation of royalties can be obtained by writing to Charlesbridge Publishing and The Global Fund for Children.

Library of Congress Cataloging-in-Publication Data
Padmanabhan, Manjula.
  I am different! / Manjula Padmanabhan. — 1st U.S. ed.
     p. cm.
  Text in sixteen different languages including English, Hebrew, Hawaiian, Cree, Arabic, Filipino, Gullah, Mandarin, Hindi, Spanish, Nahuatl, Italian, Navajo, Swahili, French, and American Sign Language. "First published in India by Tulika Publishers under the title *I Am Different!! Can You Find Me?*."
  ISBN 978-1-57091-639-7 (reinforced for library use)
  ISBN 978-1-57091-640-3 (softcover)
  1. Multicultural education—Juvenile literature. 2. Manners and customs—Juvenile literature. 3. Language and culture—Juvenile literature. 4. Picture puzzles. I. Title.
LC208.P33 2011
370.117—dc22   2010007579

Printed in Singapore
(hc) 10 9 8 7 6 5 4 3 2 1
(sc) 10 9 8 7 6 5 4 3 2 1

Display type and text type set in Triplex and Georgia
Non-Roman script set in Arial Bold, Adobe Heiti Std., Masinahikan, and Sanskrit 2003
Color separations by Chroma Graphics, Singapore
Printed and bound February 2011 by Imago in Singapore
Production supervision by Brian G. Walker
Designed by Whitney Leader-Picone
Puzzles and concept by Manjula Padmanabhan

This book celebrates differences!

In every picture, find one item that's different from all the rest—a different color, a different shape, reversed from left to right, or just asleep when others are awake!

Along with each picture puzzle, you will find the question "Can you find me?" in one of sixteen different languages. Some of the languages are indigenous to North America. This means they were spoken first in North America. Some were brought here by immigrants from around the world.

English

Can you find me?

(Kan   yoo   fynd   mee)

Nearly two billion people speak English—that's one out of every four people in the whole world. In the United States, eight out of every ten people speak only English.

אֵיפֹה אֲנִי?

Ayfo ani?

(Ay-foh   ah-nee)

Hebrew is one of the oldest written languages in the world. Classical Hebrew has been the language for prayer and study among Jewish communities around the world. Hebrew was revived as a spoken language in the early twentieth century. Modern Hebrew is one of the official languages of Israel.

Camel and hallelujah are words you might know that come from Hebrew.

Script reads from right to left

Hebre

Hawaiian

Hiki iā ʻoe ke ʻike iaʻu?

(Hee-kee   ee-ah   oh-ay   kay   ee-kay-ah oo)

The Hawaiian language has twelve letters. Only two thousand people speak Hawaiian as their native language today, but people in Hawaiʻi have started schools to teach Hawaiian to children.

Hula and ukulele are words you might know that come from Hawaiian.

ᑳᐠᒋᐢᑲᐃᐧᐣ ᒋ

Kakî-miskawin cî?

(Kuh-kee   mis-kuh-win   chee)

Cree is spoken by the Cree people, a First Nations group living mostly in Canada. Cree is the most widely spoken indigenous language in Canada.

Count to five in Cree: *peyak, nîso, nisto, newo, nîyânan.*

Script reads from right to left

Cree

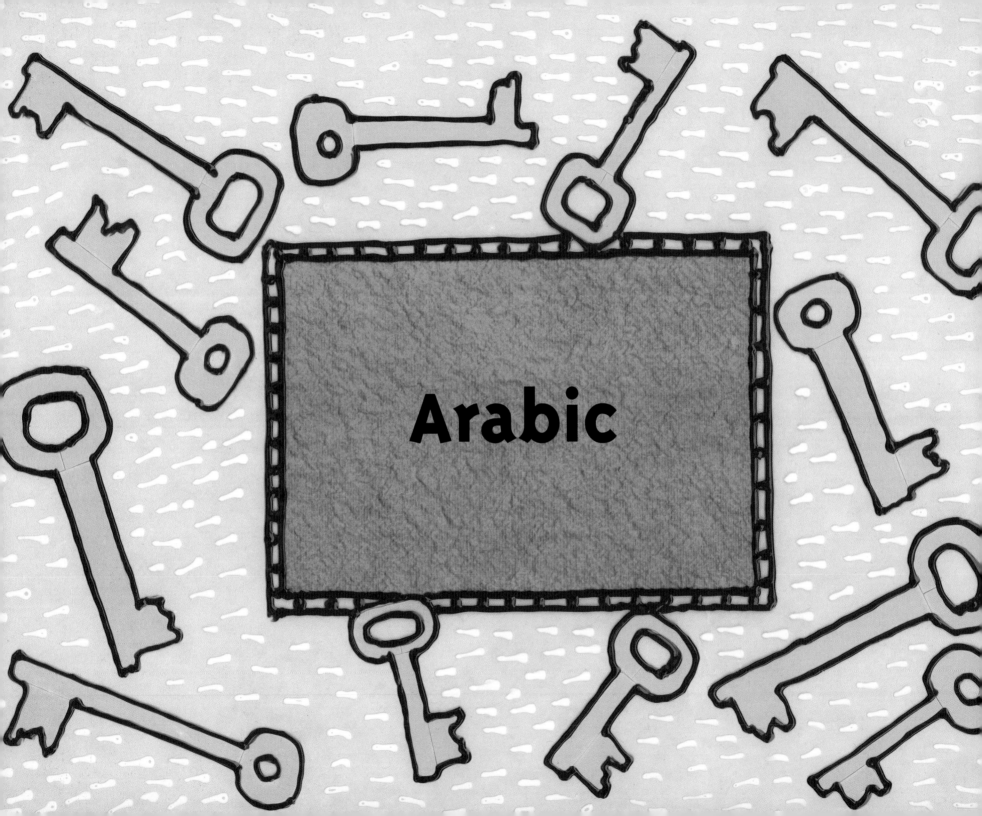
Arabic

هل تستطيع أن تجدني؟

Hael Taestaetee' an tajaednee?

(Hahl   tus-ta-tee   en   teh-jud-nee)

Arabic is one of the oldest languages in the world. Today most Arabic speakers live in the Middle East and North Africa. The Qur'an, the holy book of Islam, and many books in science and philosophy were written in Arabic.

Algebra, giraffe, and candy are words you might know that come from Arabic.

Script reads from right to left

Mahahanap mo ba ako?

(Mah-hah-hah-nahp mo bah ah-ko)

Filipino is the official language of the Philippines. It is part of a language family throughout Southeast Asia and the Pacific. Over the years it has been influenced by Spanish, English, Arabic, Sanskrit, Old Malay, Chinese, and Japanese.

Boondocks, cooties, and yo-yo are words you might know that come from Filipino.

Filipino

Gullah

Oona kin fin me?

(Oo-nuh   kin   fyne   mee)

Gullah is a creole language based on English, with strong influences from West and Central African languages. It developed as people from different African countries, who were forced to come to America as slaves in the 1700s and 1800s, had to communicate with one another in a language other than their own. Gullah is spoken mostly along the coasts of Georgia and South Carolina in the United States.

Gumbo, tote, and yam are words you might know that come from Gullah.

你 可 以 找 到 我 吗?

Nǐ kěyǐ zhǎodào wǒ ma?

(Nee   keh-yee   zhow-dow   woh   ma)

Chinese is the first language of about one-fifth of the world's population. Chinese has many spoken varieties, or dialects, but one common written language. The pronunciation shown here is based on Mandarin, or Pūtōnghuà, which means "common" language.

Silk, catsup, and Tai Chi are words you might know that come from Chinese.

Chinese

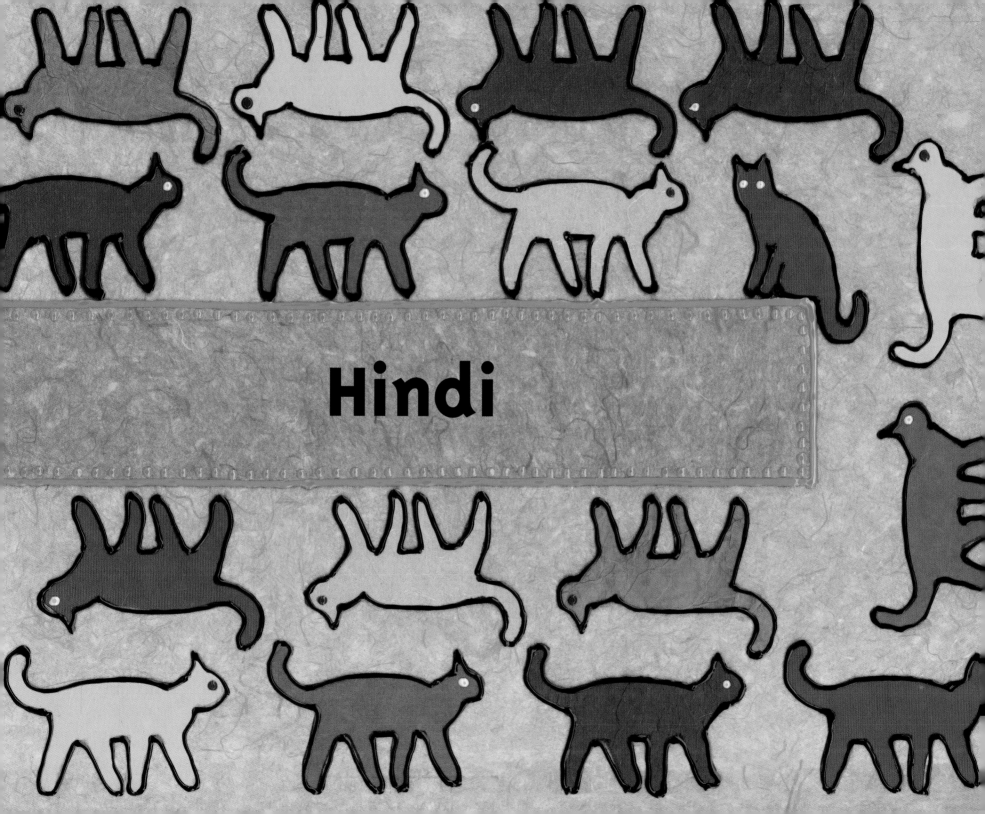

Hindi

क्या तुम मुझे ढूँढ सकते हो?

Kya tum mujhay Dhoondh saktay ho?

(Kee-yah   thum   moo-jay   doond   suck-thay   ho)

Hindi is one of the most popular languages in the world. It is the most widely spoken of India's official languages. It is spoken in nearby Nepal and Malaysia, and as far away as South Africa and Trinidad.

Cheetah, pajamas, and shampoo are words you might know that come from Hindi.

¿Me puedes encontrar?

(Meh   pweh-dehs   ehn-cohn-trahr)

Spanish is the second most widely spoken native language in the world. Most Spanish speakers live in Latin America, Spain, and the United States. Mexico has the largest population of Spanish speakers.

Alligator, hurricane, and cafeteria are words you might know that come from Spanish.

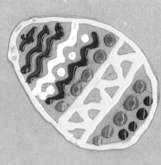

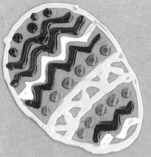

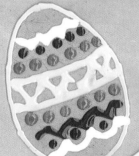

Spanish

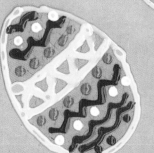

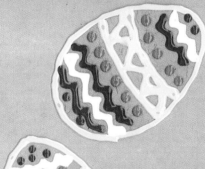

Nahuatl

Hueli tinechahci?

(Weh-lee   tee-netch-ah-see)

Nahuatl began as the language of the Aztec peoples many hundreds of years ago. Since Mexico City was the heart of the Aztec civilization, some people, especially in central Mexico, speak Nahuatl languages today.

Coyote, chocolate, and tomato are words you might know that come from Nahuatl.

Mi puoi trovare?

(Mee   poo-oy   tro-vahr-eh)

Italian is the closest modern language to Latin, the language Romans spoke two thousand years ago. Many words we use in Western music are Italian, such as *forte* (loud), *adagio* (slow), and *allegro* (lively).

Macaroni, umbrella, and volcano are other words you might know that come from Italian.

Italian

Navajo

Shíká hádíní'ii'?

(Shee-kah   hahd-in-ay-ee)

Navajo is the most widely spoken indigenous language in the United States. During World War II, a code based on the Navajo language was used to send messages over military radio.

Here are some animal names in Navajo that you can learn: *gah* (rabbit), *shash* (bear), and *ayání* (buffalo).

Unaweza kunipata?

(Ooh-nah wey-zah   coo-nee-pah-tah)

Swahili is one of the most widely used languages in Kenya, Tanzania, and Uganda. Swahili uses many words from Arabic, as well as words from English, Persian, Portuguese, French, and German.

Learn the rainbow in Swahili: *nyekundu* (red), *chungwa* (orange), *manjano* (yellow), *kijani* (green), *samawati* (blue), and *zambarau* (purple).

Swahili

French

Peux-tu me trouver?

(Peh-tyoo   meh   troo-vay)

French speakers live in France, Canada, Belgium, Switzerland, Haiti, Algeria, Morocco, and Tunisia, among other places. French is also one of the official languages of the Olympic Games.

Ballet, caterpillar, and machine are words you might know that come from French.

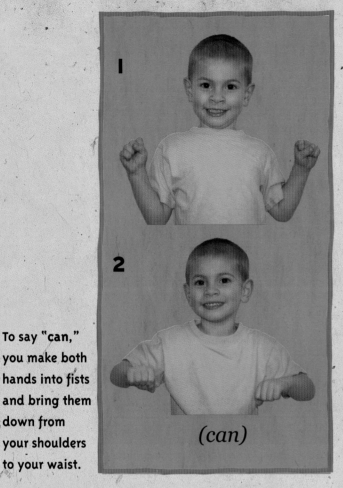

1

2

(can)

To say "can," you make both hands into fists and bring them down from your shoulders to your waist.

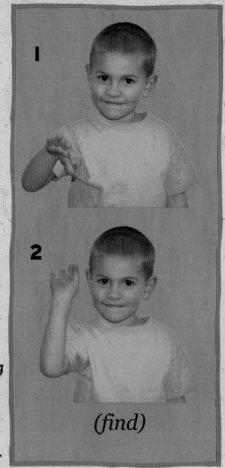

1

2

(find)

For "find," pinch the fingers of one hand like you're picking up something small, and bring your hand upward.

(you)

"You" is a pointing finger. We can tell it's a question from the look on the speaker's face.

American Sign Language, or ASL, is the most popular sign language for Deaf people in the United States. ASL has its own grammar and figures of speech like any language. Words are shown through hand position, movement, and facial expression.

What's different about this translation? We leave out the sign for "me," because in ASL, "me" means the speaker. Can you find the bird that is different on the next page?

American Sign Language

What's different?

There are many different ways of being different. It all depends on what you're looking for. These are the correct answers from one point of view. If you feel there are DIFFERENT correct answers, write and tell us!

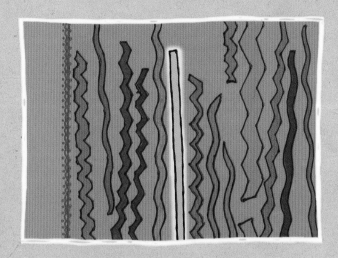

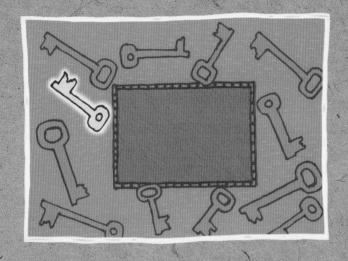

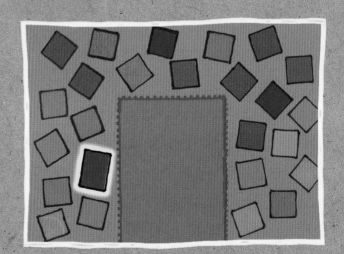

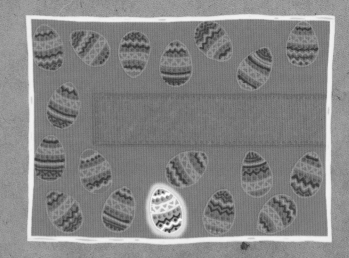

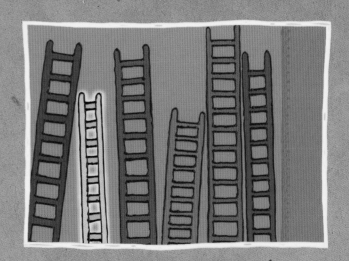

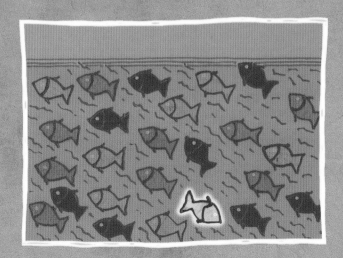

Did you know that the cover is also a puzzle? Look for the hand facing the other direction.

Languages Around the World

Language helps people connect with one another. How we name things—people, places, animals, toys, even thoughts and feelings—can create special bonds within our communities. By learning languages that are different from the ones we grew up speaking, we can better understand how others see the world. Asking "Can you find me?" in sixteen languages gives us a peek at the many interesting cultures we can find in North America and around the world.

People write languages in different ways, too. Some languages put a question mark at the end of a sentence. Others put one at the beginning and the end. Some languages are read from left to right, while others are read from right to left. Some use pictures and symbols instead of letters.

While you look for the object that's different on each page, try out the language yourself. Use the pronunciation guide underneath each sentence to help you say the words. When you say a word, what shape does your mouth make? How does it feel on your lips, tongue, or throat? How does it sound different from your own language?

Keep practicing different languages, and share this book with others, so they can try, too. You may find that "different" is just as nice as "same."